abracadabra

cello

beginner

T0337600

Katie Wearing and Frankie Henry

with Elaine Scott

Introduction

Abracadabra Beginner Cello is full of exciting games and songs to help you play your cello well – you'll learn how to sit properly, how to hold your cello, how to make the correct shapes with your fingers and how to hold the bow.

The CD has exciting backing tracks to play along with, and is great to use when you play at home. You can also play lots of the pieces with friends, who are also learning with *Abracadabra String Beginners*.

So have fun and enjoy playing your cello!

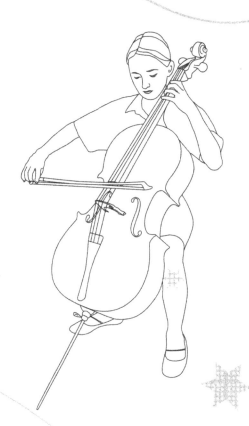

Notes to parents

The *Abracadabra String Beginners* series has been developed to cover the very important initial stages of learning a bowed string instrument. From the very start it focuses on developing good posture, and includes many games and songs which help to develop the pupil's technique as well as building general musicianship skills. It covers a wide variety of musical styles with both original and traditional songs and games that will engage pupils and encourage them to play.

The accompanying CD is ideal for making playing at home both easy and fun.

There is no longer a CD supplied with this book. All tracks are available to download from collins.co.uk/abracadabra-downloads.

Contents

Getting ready

See-saw ②

✸ This is a 'see-saw' song. Swing from your left foot to your right foot, transferring your weight to and fro. Keep your body upright but relaxed. Swing to the pulse of the music.

Hey,　ho,　here we go,　up and down and high and low.

Warm-up rap ③

✸ You need to be as relaxed as possible in order to play the cello well. Use this action rap to help you loosen up and get ready to hold your cello.

Come on kids!

Want to hold my instrument
Along with you,
And in order to get ready,
This is what we've got to do:

Shake your body to the left,
Shake your body to the right.
Stoop to the floor,
And stretch to the light. (Yeah!)

Gonna wiggle my fingers,
Gonna wiggle my toes,
Relax my shoulders,
Nice and slow.

Now if you're as ready
As you can be,
Slow down your moves
And end with me.

Fox and chickens

✸ Use this fun rhyme to find the correct position to sit with your cello.

Chick, chick, chick, chick, chicken,
(Flap your elbows like a chicken.)

Lay a little egg for me.
(Flap your elbows like a chicken.)

Chick, chick, chick, chick, chicken,
(Prepare to stand up.)

Fox is coming for his tea.
(Run around your cello like you are running away from the fox, and end sittting back down on the edge of your chair, as if you are watching out for the fox.)

✸ Whenever you see this picture in the book, check that you are sitting up straight at the front of your chair, with your feet flat on the floor – ready to jump up if the fox comes.

Strumming ⑤

✸ Now that you can find the right way to sit with your cello, you are ready to make some sounds!

✸ Move your right arm around in a big circle and as you do it, strum your fingers across the strings and listen to the sounds they make.

✸ Listen to track 5 on the CD and strum your right hand across the strings in time with the pulse of the music.

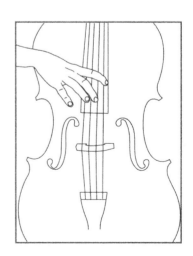

String names

★ These are the letter names of your strings:

A   D   G   C

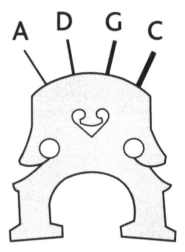

★ You might like to give them each a name, eg Anna, David ...

★ Can you make up sentences to play? Write your own to remember in the spaces below.

After   Dinner   Granny   Cooks

A_____D_____G_____C_____

LEARNING THE STRING NAMES.

Pizzicato playing

Flying pizzicato

★ Sing and play these songs using flying pizzicato. Using big circular arm movements, pluck the strings and make your right hand fly away from the cello each time.

 Skip to my Lou

D   **D**   **A**   **A**
Lou,   Lou,   skiptomyLou,   Feet arecold,   I've lostashoe,

D   **D**   **A**   **D**
Toes are i - cy,   turn-ing blue,   Skiptomy Lou, my   dar - ling.

PIZZICATO PLAYING, DEVELOPING A SENSE OF PULSE AND PRACTISING YOUR RIGHT ARM ACTION.

7

Hanukkah song ⑦

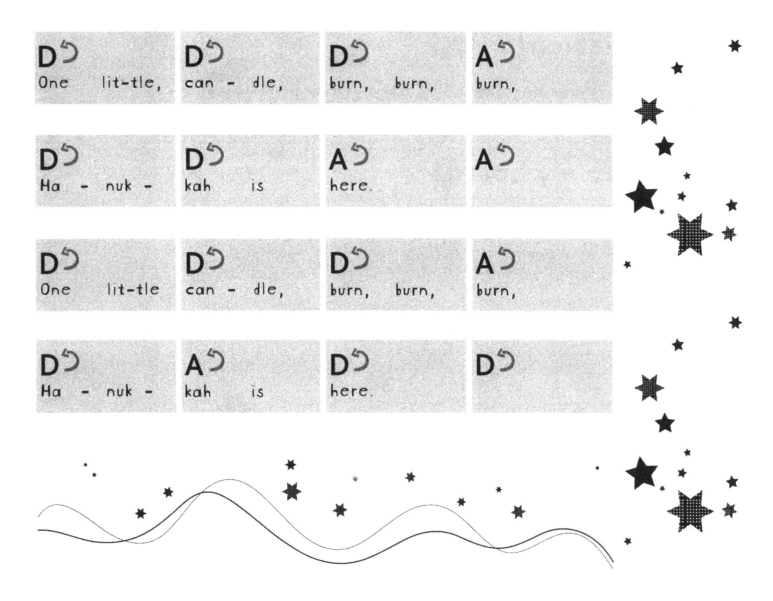

D	D	D	A
One lit-tle,	can - dle,	burn, burn,	burn,

D	D	A	A
Ha - nuk -	kah is	here.	

D	D	D	A
One lit-tle	can - dle,	burn, burn,	burn,

D	A	D	D
Ha - nuk -	kah is	here.	

DEVELOPING YOUR STRING KNOWLEDGE, SENSE OF PULSE AND RIGHT ARM ACTION.

Swing 'n' sway 8

D ⤵	D ⤵	A ⤴	D ⤵
One two three,	one two three,	swing as you	play,

D ⤵	D ⤵	G ⤵	D ⤵
Fly with your	right arm and	let your-self	sway!

Charlie Chicken 9

G ⤴	G ⤵	D ⤵	D ⤵
Char-lie Chi-cken	went a-trip-pin'	down to South Pe- ru,	He

G ⤵	G ⤵	D ⤵	G ⤵
found him-self a-	roast-in' like a	siz-zlin' bar-be- cue.	

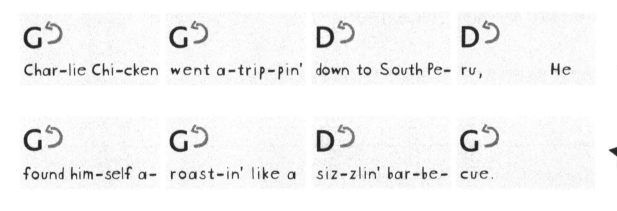

★ You can also play *Charlie Chicken* using your C and G strings.

Intercity shuttle 🔟

★ Turn your hands into express trains and fly your fingers along the tracks whilst you sing this song. Experiment with trains at different speeds.

Intercity shuttle flies along the track,
Up to the town and then straight back.

★ Now try singing the song again and pluck these strings using your flying pizzicato.

D ↻	A ↺	D ↻	A ↺
In-ter-ci-ty	shut -tle	flies a-long the	track,
D ↻	A ↺	D ↻	D ↻
Up to the	town and	then straight	back.

DEVELOPING YOUR LEFT HAND SHAPE AND YOUR RIGHT ARM ACTION.

Left hand pizzicato

★ Pluck the A string with the little finger of your left hand.

★ Pluck with fingers 4 3 2 1, 4 3 2 1, 4 3 2 1, 4 3 2 1 etc,
then try 3 2 1 4, 3 2 1 4 etc.

★ Try making up some finger patterns of your own using
each of your four fingers to pluck the A string.

★ Pluck your patterns on the other three strings.

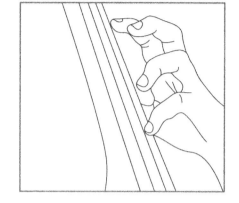

 # Autumn leaves 11

★ Pluck this accompaniment with your left hand little finger as you sing
the song with your teacher or with the CD.

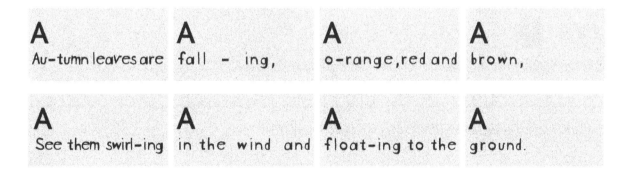

A	A	A	A
Au-tumn leaves are	fall - ing,	o-range, red and	brown,

A	A	A	A
See them swirl-ing	in the wind and	float-ing to the	ground.

Rain on the green grass

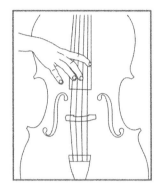

★ Sing along with your teacher or the CD, clapping the words below while you tap the pulse with your foot.

★ Pluck the rhythm of the words with your right hand while you sing. To make it easy, keep your hand close to your cello strings.

D	D D	D D	A	A A	A ⸲
Rain	on the	green grass,	rain	on the	trees,

A	A A	A A	D	D D	D ⸲
Rain	on my	head and	rain	in my	tea.

Simon says

★ Listen to the CD. Copy each rhythm Simon plucks on his A string but when you hear the *Rain on the green grass* rhythm, don't play it!

★ Can you be Simon and make up some rhythms for your teacher or a friend to copy?

Bow time!

Zoom, zoom, zoom

⭐ Sing this song with your teacher or a friend. The actions will help you to develop a good bow hold.

Zoom, zoom, zoom, we're going to the moon,
(Crouch down, placing the screw of your bow on the floor and holding it upright as if to balance it.)

Zoom, zoom, zoom, we're going very soon,
(Tap your little finger to 'pump up' the fuel. Keep your finger curved.)

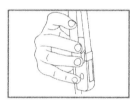

5, 4, 3, 2, 1.
(Count down 5, 4, 3, 2, 1.)

BLAST OFF!!
(Blast off upwards, then point your first finger to show where the rocket is going.)

Monkey up a tree

⭐ Make your hand climb up the bow like a monkey up a tree.

Rainbows

✹ Using the point of your bow, draw different-sized rainbow shapes in the air.

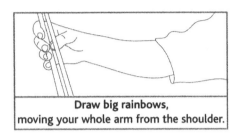

Draw big rainbows,
moving your whole arm from the shoulder.

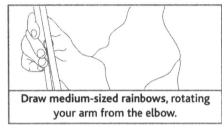

Draw medium-sized rainbows, rotating
your arm from the elbow.

Draw small-sized rainbows,
using just your little and first fingers.

Bow says 'No!'

✹ Try this with a drinking straw, and then with your bow.

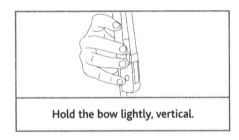

Hold the bow lightly, vertical.

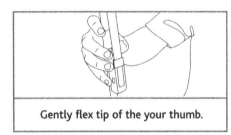

Gently flex tip of the your thumb.

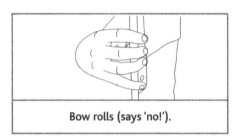

Bow rolls (says 'no!').

✹ Sing this tune and add the bow action when you sing 'No, no, no!'.

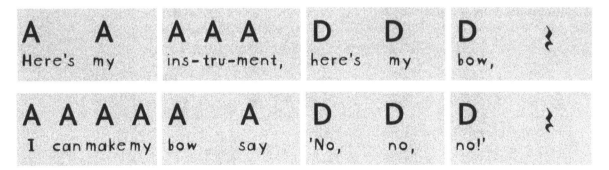

A	A	A A A	D	D	D	♩
Here's	my	ins-tru-ment,	here's	my	bow,	

A A A A A	A	A	D	D	D	♩
I can make my	bow	say	'No,	no,	no!'	

DEVELOPING GOOD BOW HOLD.

Bowing rhythms

★ Say and clap these rhythms first, then bow them on each string.

crotchet | **quavers**

A crotchet lasts for one beat. | Each quaver lasts for half a beat.

★ With your teacher, make up some new words to fit the rhythms above.

Reading notes

Rain on the green grass 🔟

★ Sing and clap the words to these songs while you keep a steady pulse with your foot. Once you have learnt the tunes, play them with long swinging bows.

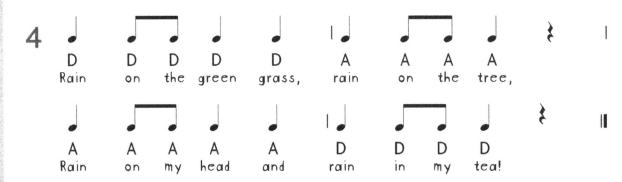

★ This is how *Rain on the green grass* looks on the stave. When you know the tune, try reading and playing it from the stave.

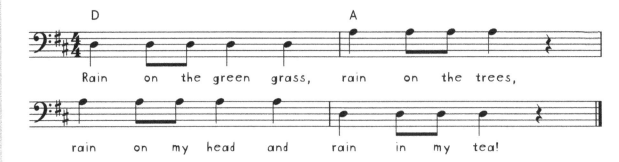

LEARNING TO READ AND PLAY FROM THE STAVE.

Ickle ockle 17 18

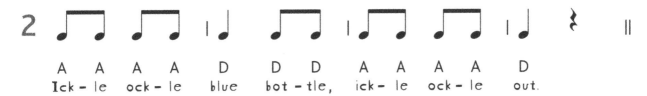

A A A A D D D A A A A D
Ick - le ock - le blue bot - tle, ick - le ock - le out.

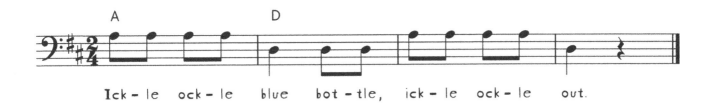

Ick - le ock - le blue bot - tle, ick - le ock - le out.

Eggs and bacon 19 20

A D A D A A A A D D A D D A A A
Eggs and ba-con in the pan, Splash, siz-zle, pop, siz-zle, then a bang!

Eggs and ba-con in the pan, Splash, siz-zle, pop, siz-zle, then a bang!

Wonky wheels  21 22

★ Sing, clap and then play *Wonky wheels* from the stave.

Won- ky wheels, my bike is slow, wob-bling is the way I go!

Invent your own!

★ Create your own bowing rhythms, choosing from

these crotchet notes: A D G C

or these quaver notes: A A D D G G C C

★ Write them in the stars, sing them, sing and clap and then play them:

Simon says 2

✴ Play *Simon says* again with the CD or your teacher.
This time Simon might use different strings, can you still copy him?
Remember to listen out for the *Rain on the green grass* rhythm.

✴ Can you be Simon? Make up some rhythms using different strings for your teacher or a friend to copy.

Who's asking?

✴ Listen carefully to your teacher or a friend, and make up answers to these musical questions:

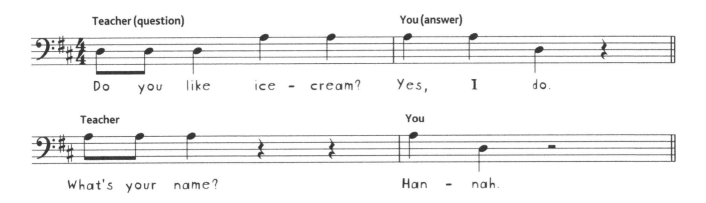

✴ Can you ask some musical questions too?

Fingers

Trampoline

★ Put your left hand 1st finger on the surface of a string, keeping it curved. Press your finger down and then lift it up again to feel the squashiness of the string. Do this a few times – it's a bit like walking on a trampoline!

★ Try this with each finger.

Faces and fingers

★ Draw a face or put a sticker on each fingernail of your right hand.
Place your fingers on the belly of your cello; then tap and say this rhyme.

Tap finger 1 - Finger 1 went to market,
Tap finger 2 - Finger 2 stayed at home.
Tap finger 3 - Finger 3 had roast beef,
Tap finger 4 - Finger 4 had none.

Open string express!

★ Put your left hand 1st, 2nd, 3rd and 4th fingers on the D string, making a tunnel for the A string express. Make up some rhythms and pluck them on your A string with your right hand, eg

All   a - board the string ex - press!

LEFT HAND FINGER SHAPES.

Harmonics

✷ Touch lightly half-way up the D string of your cello with your 3rd finger to find the harmonic: $\frac{3}{0}$

 Birds and planes 24

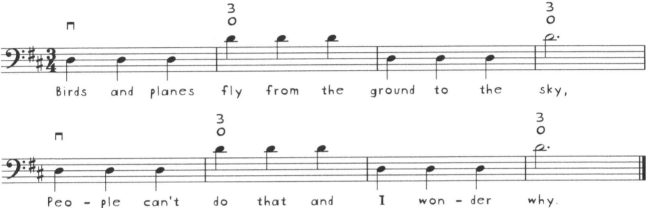

Birds and planes fly from the ground to the sky,

Peo - ple can't do that and I won - der why.

 Clever tricks 25

One, two, tap your shoe, three, four, face the door,

(tap your foot on the floor)

(turn your cello to face the door)

Five, six, cle - ver tricks, se - ven, eight, don't play late!

(touch the scroll with your left hand)

HARMONICS AND LEFT HAND FINGER SHAPE.

Number tunes

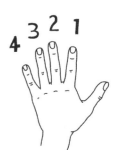

★ You can play these number tunes on any string. However when you play them with the CD or your teacher plays the piano with you, play them on the string indicated in the book. Sing the numbers along with the CD first while tapping your left hand fingers on your left thumb.

Rockbow! (CD and accompaniment = D string) 26

4 | 4 4 3 𝄾 | 1 1 3 𝄾 | 4 4 3 𝄾 | 1 1 0 𝄾

Crazy chorus (CD and accompaniment = D string) 27

4 | 3 3 4 4 | 3 3 0 1 | 3 3 4 4 | 3 3 1 0 | 1 1 3 3 | 4 4 4 4 | 3 3 1 1 | 0_0_

Grand old yorkie's duke (CD and accompaniment = G string) 28

4 | 3 1 0 0 0 0 | 0 𝄾 𝄾 0 | 1 1 1 1 | 1 𝄾 𝄾 1 | 3 3 3 3 | 4 4 4 4 | 3 3 1 1 | 0_

Tricycle ride (CD = C string and accompaniment = D string) 29

3 | 1 1 1 0 𝄾 𝄾 | 1 1 1 3 𝄾 𝄾 | 4 3 1 3 1 0 | 1 1 1 0 𝄾 𝄾

THESE TUNES HELP YOU TO MOVE YOUR FINGERS ON THE STRINGS.

African moon (CD = A string and accompaniment = G string)

4 | 0001 | 3_1_ | 02211 | 0_𝄾𝄾 | 0001 | 3_1_ | 0311 | 0_𝄾𝄾

Three beat latino (CD = A string and accompaniment = D string)

3 | 1 33 4 | 4 3 1 | 0 11 3 | 3 𝄾 𝄾 | 0 1 3 | 3 1 0 | 1 11 1 | 0 𝄾 𝄾

Can you invent your own number tunes? Write them in the boxes below.

4

3

Abracadabra!

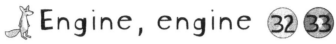 Engine, engine

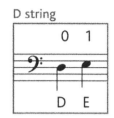

D string

En - gine en - gine num - ber nine,

Run - ning on Chi - ca - go line.

Chinese New Year 34 35

A string

Chi - nese New Year, Chi - nese New Year,

Chi - nese New Year is near - ly here.

THESE SONGS DEVELOP YOUR MUSIC-READING SKILLS.

Whirling waltz ㊱

✳ Now play *Whirling waltz* using these rhythms.

Footprints ③⑦ ③⑧

D string

0	1	3
D	E	F#

Here we go, nice and slow, mak-ing foot-prints in the snow.

Oh, how nice, once or twice, slip-ping slid-ing on the ice!

Miss Mary Mac ③⑨ ④⓪

D string

0	1	3	4
D	E	F#	G

Miss Ma-ry Mac, Mac, Mac, All dressed in black, black, black, With sil-ver

but-tons, but-tons, but-tons, All down her back, back, back.

 Ding dong! 41 42

★ This song can be played as a round, with up to four different parts. The 2nd, 3rd and 4th players start each time the 1st reaches a point marked ★.

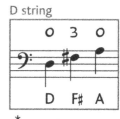

D string

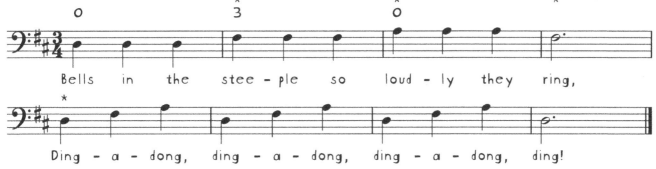

Bells   in   the   stee - ple   so   loud - ly   they   ring,

Ding - a - dong,   ding - a - dong,   ding - a - dong,   ding!

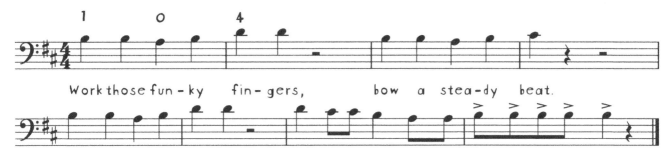 Funky fingers 43 44

A string

Work those fun - ky   fin - gers,   bow   a   stea - dy   beat.

Work those fun - ky fin - gers,   Bow with a beat from your head down to your feet.

Scale of D major

✶ You can play this as a round. The second player starts when the first player gets to *.

Invent your own

✶ Invent your own rhythms for practising the scale, eg

your favourite foods:

Sau-sa-ges and ba-con, sau-sa-ges and ba-con, sau-sa-ges and ba-con,

where you would like to go on holiday:

Ca-na-da,   Ca-na-da,   Ca-na-da,

✶ Try some others too, eg 'When is your birthday?', 'What happened this week?'

Tudor dance 45 46 47

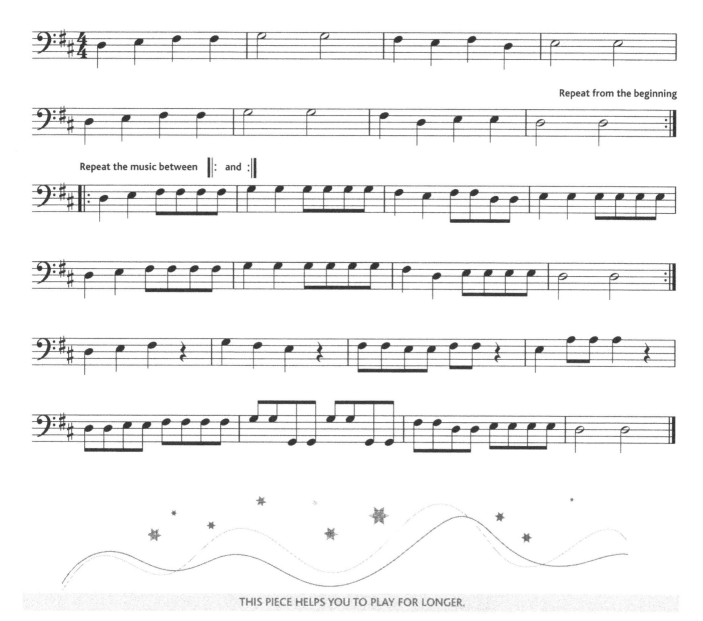

Repeat from the beginning

Repeat the music between ||: and :||

THIS PIECE HELPS YOU TO PLAY FOR LONGER.

String a simple raga

★ A raga is an Indian scale – this is an uplifting raga from South India, known as 'Hamsadavani'.

raga going up – Arohana

raga going down – Avorohana

alap – basic improvisation, in which only the raga notes are used.

raga song

Play this sim-ple ra - ga, gen-tly soothe the strings,

As you make calm mu - sic, feel the peace it brings.

PLAYING SMOOTHLY.

Goblins 50 51 52

Gob-lins, gob-lins, lots of lit-tle gob-lins!

Gob-lins are a-round to-night, ev-'ry-where you go.

Gob-lins are a-round to-night, jump-ing high and low.

If you see a gob-lin, it will scare you so!

Gob-lins are a-round to-night, ev-'ry-where you go!

pizz. (tap bow on stand)

(strum with left hand) arco

pizz. = pluck   arco = use bow

Acknowledgements

The authors and publishers would like to thank the following for their help in the preparation of this book:

Catherine Aldren, Robert Alovisetti, Adrian Bradbury, Tina Brooks, Helen Butterworth, Stephen Chadwick, Anna Cooper, Tatiana Demidova, Tim Gibbs, William Hall-Jones, Frankie Henry, Lin Hetherington, Karen Hoyle, Sebastian Imas, Sandra Isaksson, Victoria Irish, Erika Jenkins, Joan and Bernard Kenward, Harriet Lowe, Jocelyn Lucas, Chris Maybank, Doris and Christine Maybank, Alistair Mitchell, Uchenna Ngwe, Isolda Ounsted, Malcolm Pallant, Neil Pardoe, Andrew Parker, Nicholas Pegg, Marie Penny, Punitha Perinperaja, Roland Roberts, Sheena Roberts, Jane Sebba, Andy Scott, Elaine Scott, Rebecca Taylor, Katie Wearing and Emily Wilson.

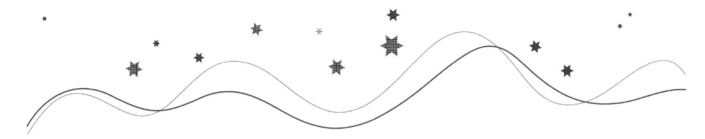

Published by Collins
An imprint of HarperCollins*Publishers* Ltd
The News Building
1 London Bridge Street
London Bridge
SE1 9GF

HarperCollins*Publishers*
Macken House,
39/40 Mayor Street Upper,
Dublin 1,
D01 C9W8
Ireland

www.collins.co.uk

© 2007 HarperCollins*Publishers* Ltd

ISBN: 978-0-7136-9366-9
Text © 2007 Katie Wearing, Elaine Scott, Frankie Henry and Chris Maybank

Audio ℗ HarperCollins*Publishers* Ltd
Edited by Neil Pardoe

Inside illustrations © 2007 Sandra Isaksson and Tatiana Demidova
Cover illustration © 2007 Sandra Isaksson
Design by Jocelyn Lucas
Music setting by Jeanne Roberts

Audio sound engineering by Stephen Chadwick 3D Music Ltd.

Printed in Great Britain by Ashford Colour Press Ltd